Key to
The Conclave
2025
and how to enter

A Disciple

First Published September 2024

First Edition

Printed and Bound in England and

the United States of America

Published by

Twelves Publications

Copyright © 2024 A Disciple

All rights reserved.

ISBN: 9798338069073

KEY TO THE CONCLAVE 2025 AND HOW TO ENTER

DEDICATED

to

The World Teacher
And disciples
everywhere

CONTENTS

	Acknowledgments	i
1	Introduction	1
2	Background	13
3	Group Meditation	27
4	Key to The Conclave - and how to enter	57
5	"We Say …"	91

KEY TO THE CONCLAVE 2025 AND HOW TO ENTER

ACKNOWLEDGMENTS

I want to express my sincere gratitude to my coworkers in our group, especially those who work tirelessly as focalisers and members of our core group. I want to mention Chandee for her assistance with the cover and Sandie, who did magical things with the editing.

KEY TO THE CONCLAVE 2025 AND HOW TO ENTER

1 INTRODUCTION

A Treatise on Cosmic Fire was an expansion of the teaching given in *The Secret Doctrine* on the Three Fires—electric fire, solar fire, and fire by friction—and it was an awaited sequence; it also presented the psychological key to *The Secret Doctrine*, and is intended to offer study to disciples and initiates at the close of this century and the beginning of the next century, up until 2025 A.D. (The Tibetan – Djwhal Khul, *Discipleship in the New Age Vol. I*, p. 778.)

Nothing is more dramatic than The Tibetan's statement regarding the impact of 2025. Written in 1925, it foretells a time when working in groups and cooperating with cosmic forces would be a natural consequence of discipleship. The Tibetan, in his cooperative effort with Alice Bailey, mentioned group working continuously and undertook work in Groups of Nine and detailed much of his efforts in the books *Discipleship in The New Age*, *Glamour, A World Problem* and *Letters on Occult Meditation* and others. The Tibetan's efforts eventually failed and he closed his group attempt. His efforts were only partially successful; however, we should consider them as precursors for post-2025.

Many of you who will read these words will do so after that momentous date, the date when the masters meet every 100 years in Conclave at Shambhala to outline the following 100-year plan. It is also the year when it is anticipated that The World Teacher will make His decision regarding Reappearance, and many of us expect that to be within the 2025 to 2050 date range as part of the externalisation of the Hierarchy generally.

The basis for our work in the New Group of World Servers (NGWS) is the teaching given to us through H.P. Blavatsky, Alice A. Bailey, and Helena Roerich. They represent the first and second phases of the externalisation of the wisdom teachings (the third phase being post-2025) and we are still determining what that will contain. Still, as practising esotericists, we can take an educated guess that it will undoubtedly include the use of symbols, sound and colour, and most of us suspect that it will be practice-based and not just another set of books. As we can see, the teachings given through those three great coworkers have been put into practice sparingly. There have been great successes, Triangles being the most spectacular. Most of us agree that Triangles set the stage for the later experimental attempts at more profound group work mentioned above.

You can research the teachings and ascertain if I have faithfully served them. I will write about what I have learned and experienced in practice. I claim nothing, and your experience in your occult practice shall be your own and will often be quite different from mine. I am not a teacher; I am an experienced esotericist in group work on behalf of our ashram and I seek to impart what little I have gathered along the way.

This book is intended for those coworkers who seek to build future groups and look for other experiences. For those without connection to esoteric group work, it may appear as fanciful nonsense. Still, to those few who seek the winding pathway to practice what they have learned in the books and to SERVE, I hope that it is useful not as a document of what to do but as a faithful testament of what has been done, tried, and tested. Naturally, the experiences related are my own and mine alone. They do not represent in any way a definitive account, as that cannot be achieved. We all have differing Dharma, Karma, Ray structure, etc., and although our way is the one pathway, we all differ in many aspects and, of course, will perceive differently when all those variables are considered.

I write this in 2024, the penultimate year to 2025. As I do so, the world is in chaos and I fervently hope that most of the restructuring has passed as you read this during and post-2025. Right now, humanity is in dire need. Wars rage, pandemics come and go, and the materialist manipulates as never before. As esotericists, we understand that the outer reflects the inner, and the forces that oppose the externalisation process will fight to create chaos and strife and promote inertia amongst coworkers.

As we know, only group work, occultly applied, can ground the cosmic, universal forces that proceed via Shamballa and

Hierarchy to our Earth. We all, all of us, have the ability to engage with and serve those spiritual forces that need representation on our planet.

We are, after all, the representatives of the Hierarchy on Earth and as members of the NGWS, we need to act and act now. The time for reading and for studying has largely been replaced with a need for action and praxis. Let us put into practice what we know, use what we have intuited, and bravely step into that magic circle of service. This small book seeks to explain and galvanise disciples to work. It sets out a simple process by which all coworkers may join The Conclave according to their ability and focus. This information has come from an initiate in the ashram who has guided the group to which I belong (a group that practices and serves The Externalisation).

I make it widely available as it can be used by all—at differing levels as all can contribute and serve to their ability.

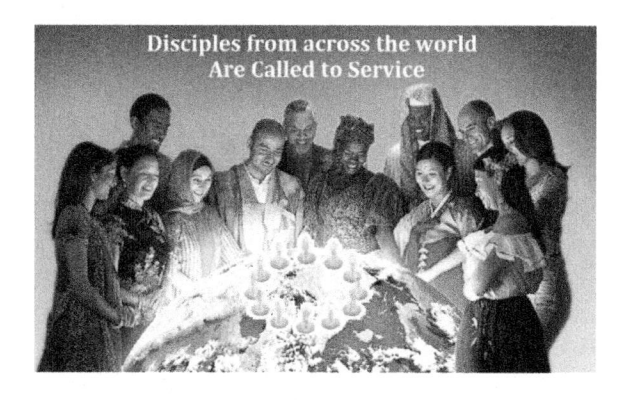

Disciples from across the world Are Called to Service

What are we, if not tenants of a cloven body entrapped by matter? And what have we become or will become as we traverse this planet unaware of our true selves? What is The Call? I write this as we hurtle towards 2024, with 2025 just a yardstick before us. To make matters short, we are part of an unfolding carpet unrolled before the universe. Nothing can stop the inevitability of the supremacy of the human soul from rising above the dross and treacle that is our incarnate state. We are truly prisoners of the planet. For where are we but immersed in the heavy weight of material concern? Does not your soul flutter when you pay it heed? Of course it does, and yet the human condition presses our soul into the muddy waters of what we call life. Life, is that what we call existence here? If you hear The Call, your soul knows differently. It knows that you are part of a greater life, a greater existence and community than your suppressed consciousness can comprehend. Your journey is not just about existence, it's about transformation and realising your true potential.

And when you have awakened, what then? Descend again into the cesspool of personality minutiae. And when you arrive at the end of your next incarnate life, what then? A great hurrah! You made it? Made what exactly? You have gotten through another incarnation. Let's race to another. What purpose do you eagerly seek for your next life, more suffering? Little did you know, before you awakened, that your goal is entwined with a greater purpose and life.

If we but know when we arrive on the inner planes and are greeted with our family and friends and we take stock and review, good and bad, where we have been, what we have done, and our victories and defeats, we must ride the horse yet again. While the thought might seem inconceivable here, once there, it is inevitable.

Having read Alice Bailey and pondered over Blavatsky and Roerich's teachings, you may wonder how to APPLY yourself to service for

The Externalisation of the Spiritual Hierarchy now underway, albeit step by step. Service is the keynote of a focused disciple who loses self in the light of service to others and our world as a whole. When we use the word service in relation to the work of the Spiritual Hierarchy, we refer to work geared explicitly towards working consciously for them. Many forms of service do not require conscious cooperation with the Hierarchy, and the vast majority of service activity in the NGWS falls into this category.

I earnestly hope that future disciples may understand the concepts and protocols behind group work, for they called and were answered. You may have questions, doubts, or even reservations, but I assure you, the answers lie within you. The Hierarchy and those who have gone before you await your commitment to service. As the Tibetan has said, "waste not time!"

2 BACKGROUND

As I sit here writing at my desk I recall, many years past, my conversation in the Great Hall with an Elder Brother of the Race who outlined the broad plan for lifting humanity from out of the mire. It was wide in breadth and scope and was more about energy currents than practical concerns. I wondered how I would play my minor part in this onslaught of lighted energy. This was long before the world wars and focused on the 100-year Conclave in

1925, a pivotal event of immense historical significance. To pierce the ugly morass takes pointed light that focuses and cracks open the veils of illusion that cloud humanity in the depth of fog.

Initiates were sent from the ashram to continue the streams of Shamballa Energy unleashed in 1625 at the 100-year Conclave and thence progressed to 1825 and the decision to allow the impact of Shamballa to progress with the outpouring of the consciousness of The World Teacher. A great soul was transported into humanity due to The Conclave, and the Theosophical Society emerged in 1875. The scene was set for the lead-up to the Conclave of 1925, which was to be, for all intents and purposes, the most critical Conclave before 2025.

The Stage of the Forerunner, described as such by The Tibetan, outlines the work of disciples during the period of 1925 to 2025. This was set in motion at The 1925 Conclave and the next phase of the teaching was released.

The Tibetan continued his work sharing and from 1919 to 1949, the second set of teachings radiated from the ashram. In 1925, *A Treatise on Cosmic Fire* was published, which was a continuation, to a large degree, of *The Secret Doctrine* published some 40 years earlier.

> I have made this practical application and the immediate illustration of the teaching anent glamour, illusion and maya because the whole world problem has reached a crisis today and because

> its clarification will be the outstanding theme of all progress—educational, religious and economic—until 2025 A.D. (The Tibetan, *Glamour: A World Problem*, p. 170.)

Three great forces of energy were unleashed in 1925. Firstly, as stated, a fresh and intense inflow of the power of The World Teacher and secondly, the stimulation of the process of mass media that leads us today to information, not always beneficial, via the Internet within seconds. This stimulation mirrors the Spiritual Hierarchy's attempts to reach humankind with instant appeal, stimulating the reaching out to the light. The third energy was from Shamballa in its nature and the most powerful of forces which, if not deftly applied, leads to wanton destruction and misery. Conversely, it can help break down the inverse wheel of materialism and dross for the disciple. This third energy was necessary to force humanity to choose light over darkness. Still, it is misapplied and we have the Middle East crisis, the Ukraine war, and potentially other crises. Also, it has led to epidemics and viruses, which are further threats to humankind.

The Tibetan outlined the triple understanding that humans must make progress towards before 2025. Otherwise, the world might not survive, and a reset is a genuine possibility. Another possibility is an 'Intervention,' and these issues, amongst others, will be decided upon at the 100-year Hierarchal Conclave during 2025, culminating at Wesak on May 12th, 2025. I think it's fair to say that only partial progress has been made in the three areas of understanding the World of

Meaning, the recognition of Elder Teachers, and the mass recognition of the Plan for Humankind. These last two points do not necessarily mean recognising the Hierarchy but accepting a divine plan for us all. Either way, how far humanity has progressed in these three recognitions is debatable.

> Above everything else required at this time is a recognition of the world of meaning, a recognition of Those Who implement world affairs and Who engineer those steps which lead mankind onward towards its destined goal, plus a steadily increased recognition of the Plan on the part of the masses. (Alice A Bailey, *Discipleship in the New Age, Vol. II*, p. 164.)

These three recognitions must be evidenced by humanity and affect human thinking and action if the total destruction of mankind is to be averted. They must form the theme of all the propaganda work to be done during the next few decades—until the year 2025—a brief space of time indeed to produce fundamental changes in human thought, awareness, and direction but, at the same time, a quite possible achievement provided the New Group of World Servers and the men and women of goodwill conscientiously serve. Evil is not yet sealed.

The spread of Christ consciousness and His *recognised* Presence with us has not yet been attained. The Plan is not yet so developed that its structure is universally admitted. Evil has been driven back; there are enough people aware of the possibility of divine enlightenment and of the interdependence (which is the basis of love) to form a potent nucleus, provided again that the inertia so prevalent among spiritual people is overcome.

> There is divine indication of coming events and a planned progress towards them, and this is already arousing interest among thinkers in many lands. However, the necessary responsive planning is still lacking. (The Tibetan, *Discipleship in the New Age Vol. II*, p. 164.)

And what of The Conclave? Here in 2024, the penultimate year of the 100-year cycle and on the cusp of culmination of the Stage of the Forerunner, what is next for humanity? Can we prevent disaster and increase the lighted way that is the externalisation of our Spiritual Hierarchy? And what of the Coming of The World Teacher? Are we to be observers or active in the coming changes? The Hierarchy has often pointed to inertia as one of the leading causes of humanities woes, even to the extent that if disciples had done more, World War II might have been avoided. If that is the case, World War III might be avoided more successfully by working together during 2025, the Year of Decision.

> Thus, a great and new movement is proceeding, and a tremendously increased interplay and interaction is taking place. This will go on until A.D. 2025. During the years intervening between now and then, very great changes will be seen taking place, and at the great

General Assembly of the Hierarchy—held as usual every century—in 2025 the date in all probability will be set for the first stage of the externalisation of the Hierarchy.

The present cycle (from now until that date) is called technically "The Stage of the Forerunner." It is preparatory in nature, testing in its methods, and intended to be revelatory in its techniques and results. You can see, therefore, that Chohans, Masters, initiates, world disciples, disciples and aspirants affiliated with the Hierarchy are all at this time passing through a cycle of great activity. (The Tibetan, *The*

Externalisation of the Hierarchy, p. 530.)

We are so close to The Conclave that it must inspire us to even greater work. As we know, group work is the future work and the easiest way for the Hierarchy to connect with and funnel to humanity those energies that will enable balance to return to incarnate life. How is this achieved in a working esoteric group? Groups will work as practical agents of light Destroying, Building, and Healing. This is a time of the sword, not the calming of the elixir.

> Shield and lance! God has blessed the warriors.
> All will come. Twilight will end.
> Do you not see that the Cosmic Consciousness is in convulsion?

> We know the course of the battle—the Plan of the Creator cannot be altered.
> From the Beginning the dark ones struggled.
> From the Beginning We conquered.

(Morya, Leaves of Morya's Garden I, p. 64.)

The dark forces, as we call them, mainly consist of discarnate beings who manipulate materialistic human beings through many means such as lust for power and possessions, and promote the grand illusion of 'there is nothing more,' the antithesis to the world of meaning. Those who manipulate the world for their nefarious means spread the lie that there are 'no consequences' to our actions, that this life is all there is so grab what you can. Their methodology is often very subtle so as not to arouse attention. They promote the 'me, me, me' culture as the pinnacle of human achievement and denigrate those seeking an alternative paradigm. Their tools include mass media, disinformation, slurs, innuendo, and cancel culture—if you do not accept it, you will be canceled as if you never existed. The rise in separative focus on race, gender, and politics is a good example. They are not highlighting our oneness but instead how different we are. Subtle is the hand of the dark one, and our planet is the battlefield between light and darkness.

KEY TO THE CONCLAVE 2025 AND HOW TO ENTER

3 GROUP MEDITATION

When meditation is discussed, people assume and visualise a picture of someone sitting in contemplation. As part of the 1925 Conclave outreach, the Tibetan was primarily responsible for introducing the active-based Occult Meditation concept. In other words, it produces 'something' that aids the forces of light. The Tibetan, who heads the Hierarchy's efforts to train and teach humanity, often tells us about the power of meditation, especially group meditation, which multiplies that which is undertaken many times exponentially.

The Tibetan has outlined that group work from its lowest form (triangles), to its highest form (one hundred and forty-four), multiplies the vortex created many thousands of times. It is difficult to quantify a neat number to accurately describe this as it depends on the quality of the coworkers engaged in the work. One hundred and forty-four trained and accepted disciples would be more valuable than a million unfocused aspirants, no matter their good intentions and goodwill.

Not only is increasing the availability of energy beneficial, but it is also far safer to undertake such work with a group of trusted coworkers. The Tibetan set up a group on the Earth plane to experiment with this concept. It eventually failed but gave us a valuable outline of its work in the *Discipleship in the New Age* books. More advanced work followed in Triangles, Nines, and Twelves and continues to this day. The work of groups had exponentially increased since the 1920s and 1930s when there were only four hundred accepted disciples on Earth, and only one hundred and fifty-six had the ability to form a group. The ashram only had a few thousand in incarnation upon the Earth:

> They, the members of the one group, are organising these forward-looking souls into groups which are destined to bring in the new era of peace and of goodwill. These latter who the group members are influencing are as yet only a few thousand among the

> millions of men, and out of the four hundred accepted disciples working in the world at this time, only about 156 are equipped by their thought activity to form part of this slowly forming group. (The Tibetan, *A Treatise on White Magic*, p. 418.)

This refers to the NGWS and the setting up of the outreach of The Externalisation. Now, nearly one hundred years later, we seek to take this group concept to the next level with a conscious group working alongside members of the Spiritual Hierarchy in incarnation and those on the inner planes.

The NGWS represents the Hierarchy on our planet, and sub-groups within the NGWS focus on particular aspects that the masters wish to advance. When joining a genuine hierarchical group, Disciples are required to focus and set aside all other things when undertaking the work. The Tibetan called it "occult obedience," however, this is not meant in any dictatorial way but in the sense of recognition of the sacrifice of service. Part of the work of genuine occult groups is setting up a funnel or vortex so that energy may be transmitted to where it is needed in the world or for some particular need of the master. Also, the work needed to help build the world Antahkarana across which the World Teacher shall tread is of vital importance. From this building of the personal and group Antahkarana, a recognition arises regarding the ultimate law of the universe: karma.

> We consider it [Karma] as the Ultimate Law of the Universe, the

source, origin, and fount of all other laws which exist throughout Nature. Karma is the unerring law that adjusts effect to cause on the physical, mental, and spiritual planes of being. As no cause remains without its due effect from greatest to least, from a cosmic disturbance down to the movement of your hand, and as like produces like, Karma is that unseen and unknown law which adjusts wisely, intelligently and equitably each effect to its cause, tracing the latter back to its producer. Though itself unknowable, its action is perceivable. (H.P. Blavatsky, *The Key to Theosophy*, 1889, p. 136.)

For the disciple, it is unquestionably known to them that the unerring Law of Karma operates dynamically every second of every day. In the group context, each coworker deals with his or her karma. However, this must be set aside for the higher group good. Hence, genuine occult groups are largely impersonal. That is not to say that a group member may not attend to a coworker in need—quite the opposite—but it does bring with it the more detached energy of observer status.

Let us talk a little about Group Initiation. The Tibetan has clarified that group initiation must be preceded by something "of enrichment to the ashram," which usually means a point of responsibility for a part of the ashram's work of externalisation. It does not mean just joining a group that demonstrates no particular focus or purpose, although such groups still contribute to the work of Goodwill in a general way. Groups who pioneer a type of work for the ashram always contain senior disciples in their ranks. The work must be group service and not an individual accomplishment—the ashram will view the group as a whole.

The NGWS contains all such groups within its Ring-Pass-Not, as the NGWS is the sole repository of the Hierarchal energies streaming into the world to stimulate externalisation.

The journey to the center of the ashram is graded by nature and each coworker achieves what his soul dictates, which can be achieved through his abilities, karma, and focus. This last point is worth highlighting, for an accepted disciple can suffer from inertia and lack of response no matter their advanced status. This happened in The Tibetan's group work, and it eventually led to the failure substantially by disciples' lack of focus in forming the very basic foundation to group work that of Triangles:

> The work has hitherto been complicated by the attitude of those who have sought to help but who have regarded it as a seriously difficult matter to form Triangles. (The Tibetan, *Discipleship in the New Age Vol II*, p. 581.)

Today in 2024, the Triangles network has spread worldwide and many thousands are engaged in this foundational White Magic work to distribute, primarily, the energy of Goodwill. A few groups attempted to advance this work into Nines (three triangles) in the 1980s, founded by Marion Walter, a controversial figure to some but a close worker with Alice Bailey.

The group had some leading esotericists, including the writer Vera Stanely Alder. Marion had this to say about 2025:

> The initiates and Masters will not emerge until after 2025, the date having been postponed because of the world war, which was not foreseen by the hierarchy when DK stated that the Masters and the Christ would emerge at the end of this century in his earliest books.
>
> The most intensive preparation will be done between now and the end of the century by disciples

from these three ashrams, or technically on the 'periphery' of these ashrams.

The work we do will make possible the emergence of a senior initiate from the second ray ashram and finally a second ray master after 2025. What a rare opportunity to serve! This process is also taking place in other planetary centres, most likely those conditioned by rays 1 and 7. The work of preparation within these planetary centres is basically to ground energy from the ashram, but it will also involve much more than that. (Marian Walter, *Applicants at the Portal*, 1954, Set 3.A-1.)

The expansion has continued with an occult group called Twelves (four triangles). This group successfully cooperates with an initiate in the Second Ray Ashram of Koot Hoomi. The work of Twelves, which is an experiment in externalising the ashram on Earth, is coupled with expanding the Triangles work laid out by The Tibetan. The group has over 150 participating coworkers and is currently active in transmitting and working with the World Antahkarana.

Please see the Twelves website for much more information: www.TwelveStar.org.

The journey to The Conclave is triple: the Journey itself, the Return or The Approach, and The Distribution (this will be explained later). The Twelves group is committed to using the techniques outlined in this book throughout 2025. The protocols are freely described here so that other groups might benefit from them in the future.

It is understood that working in groups will be how future generations interact with our Hierarchy and distribute energies throughout the planet, both during externalisation and post-externalisation. Triangles will forever be the foundational way of distribution, whilst the more advanced work in larger groups of Twelve (thirty-six, seventy-two, and ultimately one hundred and forty-four) is for those Accepted Disciples who wish to serve more powerfully. Currently, the Twelves group has several groups of thirty-six, referred to as Grand Triangles.

The ashram is an energy point usually containing a master at the head with several initiates of one of the Seven Rays. However, some decades ago at the last Conclave, it was decided to have an operational merged ashram called The Brotherhood of the Star or The Ashram of Synthesis. On the Earth plane, its reflection would be the NGWS. The combined strength of this approach is explicitly designed to ease communication and the externalisation plan. The Antahkarana would be built between Shamballa, the Hierarchy, and the NGWS.

> There were the three disciples, beloved and close; then the nine, who completed the inner Ashram [Twelve – editor]. Next came the seventy, who were symbolic of the Ashram as a whole and, finally, the five hundred, who typified those upon the Probationary Path who were under supervision by the Master but not by the three, the nine and the seventy until the time comes to admit them to the Path of Accepted Discipleship. In the greatest Ashram of all, Sanat Kumara has the same sequence of relationships among the great

> Beings Who form His group of active workers. However, remember that these figures are symbolic and not factual. The number of disciples in an Ashram varies constantly. Still, always there are the three who are responsible to the Master for all ashramic activity, who are in His closest councils and who carry out His plans. The chain of Hierarchy is great and immutable and the sequences unalterable. (The Tibetan, *Discipleship in the New Age, Vol. I*, 1931-1940, p.759.)

The Brotherhood of the Star is, therefore, an amalgamation of ashrams and The Tibetan talks of five ashrams at the centre:

Five of the Masters and Their five Ashrams are primarily involved in this preparatory work. There is, first of all, the Ashram of the Master K.H., which is the presiding Ashram in this work, owing to the fact that it is a second ray Ashram, and therefore, upon the same line of spiritual energy and descent as the Christ Himself. Another reason is that Master K.H. will assume the role of World Teacher in the distant future when Christ moves on to higher and more important work than dealing with the consciousness of humanity. Next comes the Master Morya and His Ashram, because the whole procedure is projected

> from Shamballa, and He is in close touch with that dynamic centre. The Master R., as the Lord of Civilisation, is necessarily closely involved in this preparatory work, and also because He is what has been called the Regent of Europe. (The Tibetan, *The Externalisation of the Hierarchy*, 1957, p. 644.)

The Initiate, a senior assistant to KH, is the source of the teachings concerning Twelves and this attempt at outlining the technique of approaching The Conclave during 2025. The Initiate does not head an ashram in the way that The Tibetan does but instead works as a senior assistant with special responsibility for Twelves. Therefore, he works closely with The Tibetan as he will be the one introducing the world to the final Phase Three teachings. We do not yet know what these teachings will involve, but the following is expected to be taught in group settings and applied practically in group form.

> Rhythm (flow)
> Quality (cause)
> Heat (fire)
> Light (electric)
> Magnetic force (karmic)
> Radiation (distribution, sharing)
> Activity (group work and anti-inertia)

The age of book learning is rapidly passing, and praxis will be the new way forward. On a basic level, we can see our world changing the way it delivers information, and the new generations have much less interest in book learning. This is and will be reflected on higher levels, but it is the opposite. Of course, it starts at the higher level and is reflected at the lower level.

The group I have worked with for many decades has experienced the ashram, known as The Brotherhood of the Star and other names, as energy rings approached according to each coworker's ability. In reality it is not circular, but it is the easiest way to describe it in our limited way. Each step forward enters a Wall of Light, and the Conclave is not very different. The significant difference is The Conclave is not Approached in group formation but as an individual, a triangle, a group, or many groups. To enter the ashram is through The Burning Ground, and the following diagram simplistically represents that process:

Incarnate LIFE
Outer Ring-Pass-Not / The Outer Court
Fire by Friction / Matter Activity Physical Incarnation
Solar Fire / Soul Love/Wisdom Consciousness
Electric Fire / Monad Will Spirit
The Point of Light / The World Teacher The Flaming Diamond
The Antahkarana

"O, Light of all Lights that art in the Boundless Light, remember us also and purify us!" (H.P.Blavatsky, *The Secret Doctrine Vol. II*, 1888, p.570.)

"Darkness is infectious, but Light is attractive." (Morya, *New Era Community*, 1926.)

As can be seen, the disciple enters the Three Fires to attain a deeper connection with the ashram and become more beneficial to the ashramic purpose. It should be recalled that ashrams are not there to train aspirants and disciples. They are there as points of light to focus Shamballic force and to act as an upward and downward bridge for cosmic energies. I highlight it here as there are many similarities when discussing The Conclave and how we approach it. The Tibetan encouraged his group to understand their reason for being was the Reappearance of The World Teacher.

> I gave you a group meditation which was based upon the furthering of the work of the New Group of World Servers, as they sought to prepare humanity for the reappearance of the Christ. That preparatory work is the major incentive lying back of all that I do and was the prime reason for the formation of the group in the early

> part of this century. Pioneers of this group appeared in the nineteenth century but the organisation, as it now exists, is of relatively modern days. (The Tibetan, *Discipleship in the New Age, Vol. II*, p. 232.)

Group meditation, commonly called occult meditation or esoteric meditation, is practice-driven. It is not designed to aid the practitioner but, of course, they will be aided thereby. It is intended to be of service, with the small personal self set aside. Each individual builds the Antahkarana to the soul/monad and contributes to the group energy connection to the ashram.

> See you, therefore, the necessity of eventually organising a group in

the world which will be so constituted and so carefully chosen and interiorly related that all its members are initiates, all have created their own "rainbow bridges" with understanding and accuracy, and all can now work in such complete unity that the group Antahkarana becomes a channel of unimpeded communication direct from Shamballa to the group because every member of the group is a member of the Hierarchy. (The Tibetan, *The Rays and Initiations,* p. 258.)

We have many differing types of occult meditations in the group: the traditional Full Moon, which is the foundation of our group; a Burning Ground meditation, which works to clear dross from our planet; a training for ashramic approach named The Twelve Gates Ritual; and additionally many daily Triangles. I mention this as all have one aspect in common—approaching the outer sanctum of the ashram and entering the various layers to reach the centre. All of these meditations are practical service and use visualisation extensively. All of our coworkers are well-versed in creating a group vortex to enhance the downflow of energy. It is worth noting that the energy available to us is a continuum. It is only our lack of connection that hinders its flow. The interplay of the energy within a group formation from a Triangle to a Twelve creates a flow of least resistance for the Hierarchy.

> This response comes through the recognition of identity of purpose,

of origin and of nature, but not identity in the field of expression. You can see, therefore, that an Ashram is, indeed, a very vortex of forces, set in motion by the many types of energy within the ring-pass-not of the Ashram itself. The basic principles of dualism make themselves felt as the energy of spirit makes its impact upon soul force and personality force. Forget not that a Master expresses monadic energy, whilst disciples in His group are seeking to express soul energy and are doing so, in some measure, through their love and service. To this soul energy, they add personality force which arises from their being, as yet,

> focussed in the personality life, even whilst aspiring to soul consciousness. Herein lies their usefulness from the Master's point of view and herein lies their difficulty and—at times—their failure. (The Tibetan, *Discipleship in the New Age, Vol. I*, p. 701.)

As we play our part in this massive endeavour, it would be wise to remain grounded and balanced. In these circumstances, we incarnated into this body. We have responsibilities for family, friends, health, and careers. Avoiding the aspirant's fanaticism and retaining the disciple's balanced observance is essential. We touched upon the world's Antahkarana earlier, for it is this Rainbow Bridge across which The World Teacher shall tread. Our Hierarchy, in conscious cooperation with the Devic Kingdom, continually seeks the upliftment of humanity and the Coming again of The World Teacher. This does not happen automatically. It is an essential requirement that humanity invokes this great avatar to reappear.

It is something of note to recognise that Jiddu Krishnamurti was chosen before 1925 to be the vehicle for The World Teacher, but the fanaticism of the Theosophical Society, coupled with Krishnamurti himself rebelling against his chosen role, called the experiment to 'an end.'

Krishnamurti - the vehicle for
The World Teacher until...
"the experiment was brought
to an end". DNA Vol.2

The Star shines: it steadily goes on shining: the light flows forth from all directions and all the time; just so should love toward all flow out continuously from every brother of the Star. (M.E. Rocke, *The Coming of the World Teacher*, 1917 p. 237.)

KEY TO THE CONCLAVE 2025 AND HOW TO ENTER

4 KEY TO THE CONCLAVE AND HOW TO ENTER

Personal experience, instead of 'book experience' (so beloved of esoteric students everywhere), means going there, touching, hearing, and validating. How can we know that it is true? We experience so many differing organs in daily life yet the masters teach us about 'intuition,' as it is only through the 'higher intuition' that the masters can be found.

Firstly, since the 1980s, I have used an elementary diagram (obviously inadequate in so many ways) which was helpful when our group connected with the ashram. We still use it monthly today (2024).

As a group, our journey progresses through the circles to the center of the ashram. Each coworker experiences to the best of their ability. Entry to the ashramic 'space' is not a given. One does not just go and search, knock on the door, and walk in. Ashramic space is a rarified energy source, and what an initiate would experience there is different from that of an aspirant. However, all may enter at the level of their individual evolution. So, it can be seen that each individual has a different perception of the same thing, depending on their ability.

This last point is crucial and helps explain the constant circuitous debate about whether certain teachings are from the 'master' or another source and whether all sources should be respected, and we take what we will from each.

It is true that The Externalisation is a broad sweep of many individuals of differing abilities and evolution working together in unison. There is little question that we participate and experience the same thing differently, like the ship's engineer and a sailor: both participants are on the journey, but the experiences are very different. So I describe what my experience is like and it might not be similar to yours, in fact, it is unlikely as we have outlined.

From my experience, entering the ashramic space is a meditative and intuitive practice that gradually 'lets go' of the denser outer bodies as one gets closer to the center. It is not like walking. It is 'approaching,' and as one does so, the connection increases. I have never reached the very center, but I have 'touched the hem of the garment' and received a blessing. Those more advanced than a lower-degree member such as me can advance more deeply into the 'area of senior initiates and masters.' The approach is gradual, mindful, and takes excellent focus. I have approached deeply enough to encounter our teacher, whom we refer to as 'The Initiate,' but I can proceed no further.

When one takes up the 'Thread' with a master, one is as in kindergarten and a long, long way from personal 'usefulness.' That increases over lives and initiations. Along this 'Thread,' energy passes from the 'Center where the Will of God is known' to the hearts and minds of humankind. It must be obvious how this energy can be misinterpreted. Avoiding this glamour is essential as the need to be vigilant increases as progress is made. Not only do we progress, but our challenges also increase exponentially. The energy is dual in nature—the push-down into materialism and the upward thrust towards the light.

The externalisation of The World Teacher can be aided at many levels, each contributing as they can. No judgment should be made. Contribution should be encouraged, but understanding should be retained. Some are closer to the center than others, but each may contribute. As we walk together, let us visualise being bathed in Light, love, and acceptance. Each spark is part of The Fire, so let us roar into service! Let's meditate and similarly advance into the ashramic space as we journey from the outer Ring-Pass-Not to the place where all accepted disciples have entry. From the place of Convocation, we will pass into the very outskirts of The Convocation, and who knows, some of you may gain deeper access. However deep you may go you can aid our ashram in this great externalisation work—to know is interesting, to ignore a sin, and to serve a joy.

Let us begin our journey…

Our commitment is to bring coworkers together as members of The New Group of World Servers and, by so doing, assist those who work for the Light to undertake Soul-infused energy work for Planetary healing and transformation and closely cooperate with the Forces of Spiritual Change. Individual workers contribute within the group through harmonious blending and focused effort. We further commit to approaching The Conclave in an upward progression to assist the forces of Light in the distribution of light energy and the building of the world Antahkarana. The purpose of The Conclave is the coming together of all members of our Spiritual Hierarchy to debate, share, and conclude The Plan for the coming one hundred years.

We seek to connect and cooperate with The Conclave every month throughout 2025 and beyond. Each individual will focus on their own intent to serve prior to The Conclave meditation. The individual, during meditations, should visualise all participants functioning as one Mind, one Heart, one Soul, and in accordance with the Group purpose. It is recommended that individuals lovingly care for their physical vehicles (sufficient rest, exercise, healthy foods, and pure water) so that they have the purity to receive and distribute the energies encountered. It is essential that coworkers wear comfortable, loose-fitting clothing during these meditations. A quiet environment, with no phones, pets, or humans that could disturb the genuine focus, is required. It is beneficial to prepare thoroughly and mindfully leading up to this sacred time. Subsequently, the energies should flow through and beyond you in your daily life, ensuring 2025 is a continuum.

A group of around forty trained and Accepted Disciples are meeting at a Star Gathering in Thailand at the Wesak Festival on 12th May 2025 to connect to The Conclave and further ground the energy of working in groups of Twelve. Post-gathering, we will return to our daily lives, enhanced by this connection and service activity. In addition to practical service, our group's connection with the ashram will be significantly improved. We work in conscious cooperation providing a 'Line of Least Resistance.'

If you wish to gain more information, please see the notice at the rear of the book and visit our website which is detailed there.

Some preparation is required.

You are welcome to go through the process outlined here as often as you wish as a group or individual. Our group will do so monthly at a minimum with a guided meditation on Zoom, but you are not in any way obligated to do so. This small book informs you about what some disciples are doing and, hopefully, offers you a few signposts along the way.

Regarding mediative phenomena, some of our group are clairvoyant and some clairaudient, but you should not let lights and bells disturb your practice in any way. Our master often attempts to reach us through vivid dreams, symbolic teachings and concepts and thought forms. There is rarely a remembered meeting within our ashram.

Over the decades, I have learnt to accept these 'signs' from afar with a loving embrace and move on. All genuine encounters will generate deep experience in coworkers. We can lovingly accept these and refocus on our task.

The Conclave can be represented in two-dimensional terms, much like the ashram, as concentric circles that decrease in size until the centre is reached. It must be remembered that this is a fundamental and simplistic view of an energy mass, but it has proven helpful over many years in describing the inward journey. All our ashramic energy work is progressive towards a point of light.

Great Beings such as Avatars, Archangels, and Masters represent an energy centre, devic or human. We ourselves are an energy centre too, of course, and as we evolve and grow we become more useful within our ashram and our energy becomes more focused.

As I recorded earlier, each coworker can progress through the ring-pass not according to their evolution but according to their usefulness to the master and the work. Invocations are used at every stage to protect, invoke, and distribute the energy encountered, each according to their ability.

The six stages are:

Humanity,
Humans who practise Goodwill,
NGWS,
Disciples,
The Convocation and
The Conclave.

There are four major stages to occult group work: (1) alignment with the soul and setting aside the personality life, (2) group integration, brotherhood, and fusion in the "circle of living points of light" [DK], (3) recognition and dedication to the group purpose, and lastly (4) linking with all other groups in the New

Group of World Servers, of which every genuine group is a part.

We shall utilise six mantrams on our journey to The Conclave and a Ceremony of Protection before we start:

Ceremony of Protection

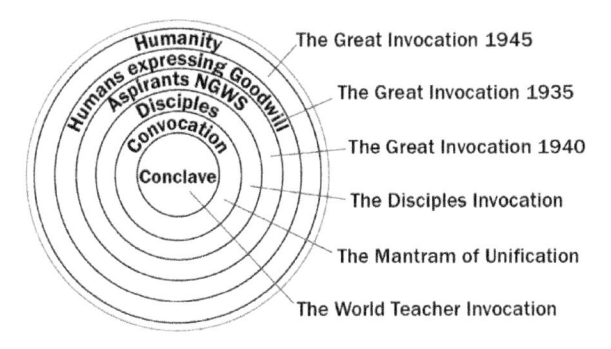

- The Great Invocation 1945
- The Great Invocation 1935
- The Great Invocation 1940
- The Disciples Invocation
- The Mantram of Unification
- The World Teacher Invocation

(Concentric circles from outer to inner: Humanity expressing Goodwill — Humans Aspirants NGWS — Disciples — Convocation — Conclave)

Standing in the Light

Let us now Stand Together before we start our journey. This entails standing outside the energy field, which is The Conclave in its broader sense. Visualise a box at your feet and place those things you will not need on your journey—family, career, health, financial concerns, etc.—in that box for collection later when you return.

Recite The Ceremony of Protection

Ceremony of Protection – adapted

We place an unbroken circle of protection about us.

We seek the Protection of our Ashram.

And in the Name of The World Teacher we Invoke the Blessing and Protection

of the Overlighting Deva and the Lords of Love.

OM OM OM

Beginning The Journey - Humanity

1. Enter The Sacred Space

This requires individuals to be fully responsible. Apart from the cautions about drugs, alcohol, etc., being incompatible with the work, coworkers need to be ready with intent. This means preparation at least three days before starting The Journey and adhering to the right action in one's daily meditations and invocations.

A calm, focused mind is required for this work. Most importantly, set aside all personal issues at the door in the box as described. Be aware that the space you are entering is now a sacred space.

Assuming that the worker is able to maintain focus and is trained in the art of being emotionally and mentally still, has read and understood these guidelines, and has set aside personal issues while undertaking this service activity, the coworker can move on to the next stage.

2. Stand in the Light and the Circle of Protection

Protection is invoked whenever group work is undertaken under the auspices of the Ashram. So, in a larger group setting such as the Conclave, we can be assured of protection for the group and individuals. It is helpful to visualise the whole group present and standing in the Light, with coworkers outlined and surrounded by light rather than as a specific person, male or female, etc.

Please take a moment to fuse with humanity as it claws its way to the light. Do not overfocus on this but recognise yourself or your group as part of humankind.

Recite The Great Invocation 1945

The Great Invocation 1945

From the point of Light within the Mind of God
Let light stream forth into the minds of men.
Let Light descend on Earth.

From the point of Love within the Heart of God
Let love stream forth into the hearts of men.
May *Christ return to Earth.

From the centre where the Will of God is known
Let purpose guide the little wills of men
The Purpose which the Masters know and serve.

From the centre which we call the race of men
Let the Plan of Love and Light work out
And may it seal the door where evil dwells.

Let Light and Love and Power restore the Plan on Earth

OM OM OM

Also known as The World Teacher, Maitreya, The Bodhisattva, the Kalki Avatar, etc.

Visualise a great Wall of Light before you or your group and step through this light as it falls upon you.

Continuing The Journey – Goodwill

Pause to reflect upon the power of Goodwill, the simplest expression of Love and the easiest for the masses to identify with. Breathe in the Power of Goodwill and Right Human Relations. Goodwill is compassion in action for all levels on our planet including minerals, vegetables, animals, and humans.

Recite The Great Invocation 1935

The Great Invocation 1935

Let the Forces of Light bring illumination to mankind.
Let the Spirit of Peace be spread abroad.
May men of goodwill everywhere meet in a spirit of cooperation.

May forgiveness on the part of all men be the
    keynote at this time.
Let power attend the efforts of the Great Ones.
So let it be, and help us to do our part.

OM OM OM

Visualise the Wall of Light before you and step through it, emerging to the other side.

Continuing The Journey – NGWS

Visualise a further wall of light shimmering with golden hues and step through that light into the energy of the New Group of World Servers. Sense the upliftment of being amongst your coworkers in their millions. Above the hue and cry of incarnate life is stillness and unity. Take your time to connect with those you know and those you do not yet know, for all are one.

Recite The Great Invocation 1940

<u>The Great Invocation 1940</u>

Let the Lords of Liberation issue forth.
Let Them bring succour to the sons of men.
Let the Rider from the Secret Place come forth,
And coming, save.

Come forth, O Mighty One.

Let the souls of men awaken to the Light,
And may they stand with massed intent.
Let the fiat of the Lord go forth:
The end of woe has come!

Come forth, O Mighty One.

KEY TO THE CONCLAVE 2025 AND HOW TO ENTER

The hour of service of the saving force has now arrived.
Let it be spread abroad, O Mighty One.

Let Light and Love and Power and Death
Fulfill the purpose of the Coming One.

The WILL to save is here.
The LOVE to carry forth the work is widely spread abroad.
The ACTIVE AID of all who know the truth is also here.

Come forth, O mighty One, and blend these three.
Construct a great defending wall.

The rule of evil NOW must end.

OM OM OM

The Wall of Light is before you—step through it.

Continuing The Journey – Disciples

You now arrive at the place of accepted disciples, and if you have the ability to see and connect with the millions therein, then know you are a disciple yourself. If you find this challenging, let it inspire you onward. Those who have committed to the externalisation plan are gathered here. Take time to pause in this fantastic place and become one with those members of the NGWS who consciously work for Hierarchy. This is the stepping stone to the outer sanctum. This group was given The Disciples Invocation in 1982 to focus on those leading the new experiment in externalising the ashram. It must be recalled that this is a world invocation that any individual or group can use.

Recite The Disciples Invocation

<u>The Disciples Invocation</u>

May the Flame of the One find the Crucible of your being
May the Mighty One issue forth from on High
May Love eternal and Love inclusive rule over all

Let the Flame spin upon the Way
Let the Light stand revealed
Let the seeker become the Rose

May the tide of illusion be turned
May the Great Work be completed
May the White Ones issue Their Ultimatum

Let the Ultimatum be heard by those who have ears to hear
Let them have insight and knowledge that they may understand
Let them choose aright and with free will

And in so choosing let Peace come to Earth

OM OM OM

And before you is the Wall of Light that leads to the Outer Sanctum of The Conclave.

The Journey to the Outer Sanctum – The Convocation

The Convocation is the meeting place for all coworkers, human and angelic/devic, incarnate and discarnate, and has many millions in attendance on the outskirts of The Conclave. The sacred space sits just before the great and last Wall of Light leading to The Conclave itself. Only those who have reached a certain degree of attainment and are accepted as disciples by a master may gather here, and only fewer may enter The Conclave itself, which lies behind the Great Ring-Pass-Not. And yet all members of The Great Council (in 2025 named The Conclave) meet their ashramic disciples in this place and merge their energies with every being here gathered. Take a moment to immerse yourself in the energies, the beauty, and the stillness.

Recite The Mantram of Unification

Mantram of Unification

The sons of men are one, and I am one with them.

I seek to love, not hate;
I seek to serve and not exact due service;
I seek to heal, not hurt.

Let pain bring due reward of light and love.
Let the soul control the outer form, and life, and all events
And bring to light the love that underlies the happenings of the time.

Let vision come and insight.
Let the future stand revealed.
Let inner union demonstrate and outer cleavages be gone.
Let love prevail. Let all men love.

OM OM OM

And before you is the final Wall of Light stretching into infinity, shimmering gold, and every hue, both imagined and unimagined in your incarnate state. When you visualise entering The Conclave, do so 'as if' you are there. Recall that the whole process, as described here, is part of The Conclave as a whole, and you will advance in your meditation as your ability allows. What is very sure is that you will share in the bountiful gifts from the masters as they are transmitted vertically and horizontally.

The Journey to the Inner Sanctum—The Conclave is a term used to describe a gathering of spiritual masters, initiates, and angelic beings. It is a place of profound spiritual learning and growth, where advanced teachings are imparted, and energies are transmitted for the coming hundred years.

KEY TO THE CONCLAVE 2025 AND HOW TO ENTER

This is the inner sanctum of the 100-year Conclave of our Spiritual Hierarchy. Members of the fifth degree are a select few, and accepted disciples who have taken the third degree may observe and assist in transmitting the energies at play here. It is a privilege to be part of this exclusive gathering.

> Occasionally (usually once in a century after Their Conclave at the close of the first quarter), there is the imparting of a more advanced body of teaching. This teaching will only be recognised by a few of the foremost disciples in the world; it will, however, prove to be the ordinary form of occult teaching during the next developing cycle. (The Tibetan – Djwhal Khul,

Discipleship in the New Age Vol. II, p. 319.)

The decisions taken here will apply to humanity for the next one hundred years. Also, the great offices of our Hierarchy are decided upon. These decisions do not affect the minutiae of our incarnate existence, and human free will is never intruded upon. The decisions concerning the Great Cycles of Energy are wide-ranging and of utmost importance. The date the World Teacher emerges and the pace of the externalisation plan will also be decided. We can know very little of these sharings amongst our teachers as we await the Third Phase of the teachings post-2025.

Recite The World Teachers Invocation

The World Teachers Invocation

Great Lord of Light - Hear our Prayer

Come aid us in our hour of need.
Come lead us to Thy Holy Fire.
Come heal our broken world.

As it has been written, so shall it be.

OM OM OM

Give Thanks

After you have completed your journey to this sacred place, give thanks to those beings with whom you have interacted. It is time to return to your incarnate state where your physical body rests.

Step back from engagement and feel yourself slowly returning to your incarnate body. Visualise the box at your feet and take the things you need. Feel free to leave those things that are no longer helpful to you in the box, which will dissolve over time into the ether.

Step back and breathe deeply—your work is done.

KEY TO THE CONCLAVE 2025 AND HOW TO ENTER

KEY TO THE CONCLAVE 2025 AND HOW TO ENTER

5 "WE SAY …"

See it, the blue star is atop the mountain!
Hear the tone of the Ashramic Bell,
Note the aroma of the Flowers of the
    Master's garden,
Feel the lighted touch of the Devic Beings
    abound,
Onward into the lighted way…

We teach, become the valiant Chevalier,
Stand the ground of the certain,
Become the Living Stones in the walls of
    our temple,

Fire is thy way,

The Great Battle has commenced,

Act, now is the hour,
Now is the moment,
Now has The Call gone forth.

Come Mighty One, Come!

Now into the three Planes of Fire step we
Let the Three Fires of Agni Burn
And Petalled Lotus unfold unto the dawn

Builders of Bridges
Lighters of Fires
Quenchers of Thirst
Unite!

Let the Call sally forth
Come Mighty One, Come!

And into the depths smote we the sullied
    one
To arise once more cleansed and mute
Humanity dressed in garb of despair
Arise!

We impart, the illusion of temporary
    distain must asunder be
You are infinite being, an eternity locked in
    diversity

The Fiery Bird has arisen
Three crowned heads has she
Yellow, Red and Fiery Gold pours forth –
    the Living Flame of the One
See you not above the heads of the
    Acolytes?

The Initiate, July 2021

KEY TO THE CONCLAVE 2025 AND HOW TO ENTER

KEY TO THE CONCLAVE 2025 AND HOW TO ENTER

www.twelvestar.org/twelves-gathering-2025

Other Twelves Books

Available on www.twelvestar.org/books

Spiritual Changemakers by Isobel Blackthorn

Esoteric Apprentice by Steven Chernikeeff

2025 and the World Teacher by Steven Chernikeeff

Discourses by The Initiate

All Alice A Bailey's books
Are available from:

Lucis Trust, Suite 54, 3
Whitehall Court, London
SW1A 2EF UK

www.lucistrust.org

KEY TO THE CONCLAVE 2025 AND HOW TO ENTER

Printed in Great Britain
by Amazon